Break That Code

Lisa Thompson and
Sharon Dalgleish

CHELSEA HOUSE
PUBLISHERS
A Haights Cross Communications Company

This hard cover edition first published in 2005
by Chelsea House Publishers

Copyright © 2003 Sundance Publishing

Published by
Sundance Publishing
P.O. Box 740
One Beeman Road
Northborough, MA 01532–0740
800-343-8204
www.sundancepub.com

Copyright © text Lisa Thompson and Sharon Dalgleish
Copyright © illustrations Matthew Lin and Cliff Watt

First published 2002 by
Blake Education, Locked Bag 2022, Glebe 2037, Australia
Exclusive United States Distribution: Sundance Publishing

Design by Cliff Watt in association with
Sundance Publishing

Break That Code
ISBN 0-7910-8427-2   CIP applied for

Photo Credits
p. 9 Image courtesy of Royal Blind Society;
p. 14 © Cliff Watt;
p. 15 photolibrary.com;
p. 25 Mary Evans Picture Library;
p. 26 © AAP Image/Alan Porritt;
p. 28 AFP/AAP/HO HO

Table
of Contents

Code Breaking Made Easy

The treasure is behind the locked door!

You've come halfway around the world on a treasure hunt. Now the only way to unlock the door to the hidden treasure is to crack these codes. How will you do it?

···−−−··· **Means SOS**

When you think of a **code**, do you imagine a spy sending a secret message? Not all codes are meant to be secret. Morse code, developed in the 1800s, once was the only way to send messages around the world. Morse code used short and long electrical signals sent by **telegraph**. The sounds were received as dots and dashes that represent letters. Telephone, fax, and computer messages have replaced Morse code. But SOS still means "Send help!"

Samuel Morse (1791–1872)

•−−/•/•−••/−•••/−•−•/−−/−•

How to Crack Code 1

To unlock the door on page 4, you must crack the three codes on the door panels. The first one, shown here, is written using Morse code. Use the **key** on the next page to crack it.

6

Sending a Message by Telegraph

- Pressing quickly on the telegraph key sends a short electrical signal, written as a dot.
- Pressing the telegraph key three times longer sends a long electrical signal, written as a dash.
- The pause between letters lasts as long as one dash.
- The pause between words lasts as long as two dashes.

Telegraph key

International Morse Code Key

A •–	K –•–	U ••–	4 ••••–
B –•••	L •–••	V •••–	5 •••••
C –•–•	M ––	W •––	6 –••••
D –••	N –•	X –••–	7 ––•••
E •	O –––	Y –•––	8 –––••
F ••–•	P •––•	Z ––••	9 ––––•
G ––•	Q ––•–	0 –––––	
H ••••	R •–•	1 •––––	
I ••	S •••	2 ••–––	
J •–––	T –	3 •••––	

Panel 1
answer:
welcome

7

Decoding by Touch

Blind people can read and write using a well-known system called Braille. Letters, numbers, and punctuation marks are replaced by a pattern of raised dots—with 63 possible combinations. Blind people can feel the raised dots with their fingers to spell out words. The code was developed by Louis Braille, who was blind himself. He experimented for three years before unveiling the code in 1824. He was just 15 years old!

The bumps on your head tell an interesting story.

How to Crack Code 2

Here is the message on the middle door panel on page 4. It is written using the Braille system. Here the message is in colored dots instead of Braille's raised dots. Crack it using the key on the next page.

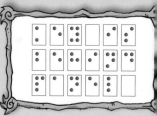

Louis Braille
(1809–1852)

The red circles show the raised dots

a b c d e f g h i j k l m

n o p q r s t u v w x y z

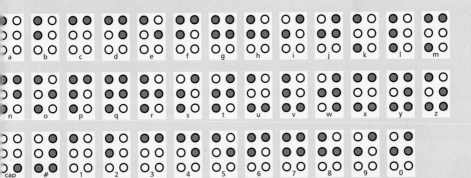

cap # 1 2 3 4 5 6 7 8 9 0

In a Spin

If the work of a **cryptographer** [crip-TOG-ra-fer] sounds mysterious, that's because it is. A cryptographer is a person who makes and breaks codes. Leon Battista Alberti is one of history's most famous cryptographers.

Leon Battista Alberti (1406–1472)

Alberti was an Italian architect and mathematician who lived in the fifteenth century. He invented the Alberti disk, a kind of coding wheel. Since its invention, the Alberti disk has been one of the most popular **encoding** methods in the world.

How to Crack Code 3

The message on the bottom door panel on page 4 is written using the Alberti disk shown on the next page. Use it to crack the last of the coded messages!

ZXQP JSL
YKEYJOTFS
ZUQSS ZTDSF

How to Make an Alberti Disk

1. Draw a large circle and a smaller circle on a piece of cardboard. Cut them out.
2. Around the edge of the smaller circle, write the 26 letters of the alphabet in alphabetical order.
3. Around the edge of the larger circle, write the 26 letters of the alphabet in **random** order.
4. Attach the smaller circle to the larger circle with a brad.
5. Move the circles so the **a** of the inner circle lines up with any chosen letter on the outer circle. Keep the disk in this position while you write your secret message. Make sure that the person decoding your message has a disk exactly like yours, with the **a** in the same position.

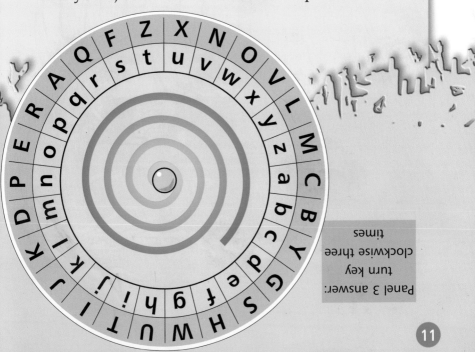

Panel 3 answer:
turn key
clockwise three
times

11

Codes In Pictures

You see a ship and your heart fills with terror.

It's flying Blackbeard's flag! In the 1600s, pirate flags used simple picture codes. On Blackbeard's flag, the skeleton holding an hourglass means, "Your time has run out!" Some more ancient picture codes are not so easy to break.

Mayan Messages

Between 700 B.C. and 400 B.C., the Maya of Mexico developed a complex system of writing. It used about 800 picture signs, called glyphs. But because no one today writes like the ancient Mayan people, the glyphs look like a great secret code.

Palace at Palenque, Mexico

Archaeologists and other scientists have been trying to break the code for many years. So far they have **decoded** nearly 85 percent of known glyphs.

Mayan glyphs, Palenque

How to Read Mayan Glyphs

Mayan glyphs can be words or syllables. Different glyphs were put together in a block to make sounds, words, or ideas.

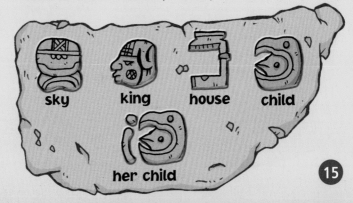

sky   king   house   child

her child

A Picture Code That Was Hard to Crack

The ancient Egyptians didn't just leave mummies and giant pyramids behind them. They also left a mystery. When their writing was first discovered, no one could figure out how to read it. Hieroglyphs (HIGH-ro-gliffs) are mostly made of pictures of natural or man-made objects. Hieroglyphic writing is one of the oldest forms of writing in the world. It was used from about 3200 B.C. to A.D. 394.

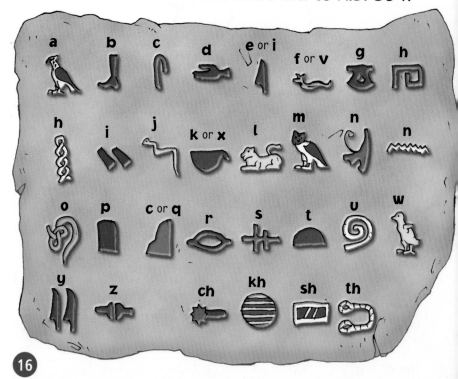

Q: Why do mummies make good spies?
A: They're good at keeping things under wraps!

Hieroglyphs carved on an ancient Egyptian building

A Stone Key

In 1799, the Rosetta Stone was found in Rosetta, Egypt. It had the same message written on it in Egyptian hieroglyphs and in Greek. Since the code breakers could read Greek, they knew they had found the key to the hieroglyphic code. But many scientists struggled for years to match each Greek letter with a hieroglyph. Then in 1822, Jean-François Champollion cracked the code. How did he do it? He realized that some hieroglyphs stood for sounds, some for syllables, and some for ideas.

How to Read Egyptian Hieroglyphs

Hieroglyphs were mostly written in rows from right to left, or in columns from top to bottom. But sometimes, if it looked better, they were written from left to right.

To tell which way to read hieroglyphic writing, look at the direction the animals or people are facing. They always face toward the beginning of the line.

The Rosetta Stone

Top Script
Egyptian hieroglyphs

Middle Script
Egyptian demotic script (a late cursive form of hieroglyphs)

Bottom Script
Greek

Secret Spy Codes

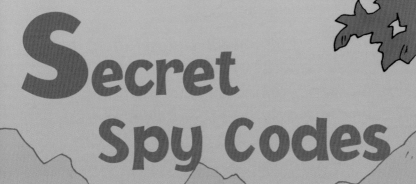

You are a secret agent on a special mission.

It doesn't matter if you lived in 404 B.C. or if you live today. If your country is at war, lives will depend on you! So what code can you use to keep your secrets safe?

A Last-Minute Warning

In 404 B.C., a messenger staggered up to the Greek general Lysander (lie-SAND-er). Five messengers had set out from Persia. This was the only one to survive. The messenger handed his belt to Lysander. Inside the belt was a meaningless line of letters. But when Lysander wrapped the belt around a **scytale**—a baton, or stick—the letters lined up and a message appeared. It said that the Persians were about to attack. Lysander prepared for battle, and won!

How to Use a Scytale

The person who writes the message and the person who reads it must have the same sized batons. You could use a cardboard cylinder instead of a baton and a long strip of paper instead of a belt.

1 Wrap the paper around the scytale. Write the message.

2 Unwrap the paper to make a meaningless line of letters.

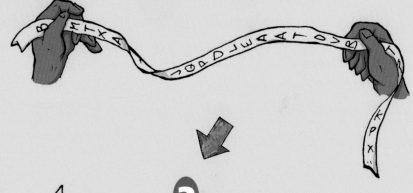

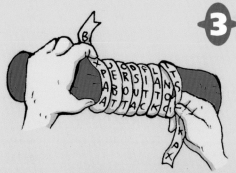

3 The message reappears when the strip of letters is wrapped around another baton or cylinder of the same size.

Secret Letter Scramble

Julius Caesar was a very famous and successful Roman general in ancient times. His armies usually won their battles because Caesar was good at planning what his troops should do next. When Caesar sent a message to tell his troops what to do, he didn't want his enemies to be able to read it. So Caesar invented his own secret code—the Caesar **cipher**.

How to Use a Caesar Cipher

In a shift cipher, each letter of a message is shifted ahead a specific number of letters in the alphabet. In this Caesar cipher, for example, each letter of the message is replaced by the letter three places further down in the alphabet. This means **a** becomes **D, b** becomes **E,** and so on. So the key to this Caesar cipher looks like this:

a	b	c	d	e	f	g	h	i	j	k	l	m
D	E	F	G	H	I	J	K	L	M	N	O	P

n	o	p	q	r	s	t	u	v	w	x	y	z
Q	R	S	T	U	V	W	X	Y	Z	A	B	C

Use the key to figure out this urgent message:
ZH ZLOO DWWDFN DW PLGQLJKW!

We will attack at midnight!
Answer

The Enigma Machine

Imagine a machine that looks a little like a typewriter, but can code a message in more than a billion ways. Meet the Enigma machine. During World War II, Germany used Enigma machines to send secret messages. To make the code even harder to break, the Enigma machine settings were changed every day.

Britain had 7,000 cryptographers working day and night to decode the Enigma messages. Finally, they were able to build a decoding machine. Their work played a large part in defeating Germany.

How to Send an Enigma Encoded Message

1. Check the code book for today's setting.
2. Change the scramblers on the Enigma machine today's setting.
3. Type the message using the keyboar
4. As each letter is typed, a different code letter will li up on the top alphabet. Write down these code letters to make th secret message.
5. Send the message by telegraph in Morse code.

Not moos code, MOR code!!

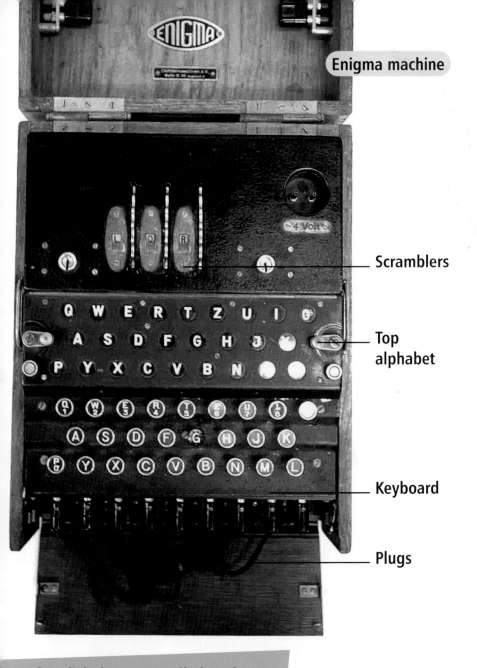

Enigma machine

Scramblers

Top alphabet

Keyboard

Plugs

Q: Why did the spy pull the sheets over his head?
A: *He was an undercover agent.*

Navajo Code Talkers

One of the codes used by the United States during World War II didn't need complicated machines. It was based on the Native American language of the Navajo. In just minutes, Navajo people, called Navajo code talkers, could send and receive a message that took half an hour using a coding machine. People trying to break the Navajo code found it hard to even write down the sounds. The Navajo code talkers' code was never broken!

The enemy will *never* decode this!

THE NAVAJO ALPHABET CODE

A	Ant	*Wol-la-chee*	**N**	Nut	*Nesh-chee*
B	Bear	*Shush*	**O**	Owl	*Ne-ahs-jsh*
C	Cat	*Moasi*	**P**	Pig	*Bi-sodih*
D	Deer	*Be*	**Q**	Quiver	*Ca-yeilth*
E	Elk	*Dzeh*	**R**	Rabbit	*Gah*
F	Fox	*Ma-e*	**S**	Sheep	*Dibeh*
G	Goat	*Klizzie*	**T**	Turkey	*Than-zie*
H	Horse	*Lin*	**U**	Ute	*No-da-ih*
I	Ice	*Tkin*	**V**	Victor	*A-keh-di-glini*
J	Jackass	*Tkele-cho-gi*	**W**	Weasel	*Gloe-ih*
K	Kid	*Klizzie-yazzi*	**X**	Cross	*Al-an-as-dzoh*
L	Lamb	*Dibeh-yazzi*	**Y**	Yucca	*Tsah-as-zih*
M	Mouse	*Na-as-tso-si*	**Z**	Zinc	*Besh-do-gliz*

How to Send a Navajo Encoded Message

The Navajo code talkers used the alphabet code above
to spell out some words.

1. Spell the words using the alphabet code. For example,
   spell 'Pacific' as 'pig/ant/cat/ice/fox/ice/cat'.
2. Translate the alphabet code words into Navajo.
   For example, translate the spelled-out 'Pacific' as
   'bi-sodih/wol-la-chee/moasi/tkin/ma-e/tkin/moasi.'
3. Transmit the message.

Decode this Navajo message:

Than-zie/Lin /Dzeh
Dzeh/Nesh-chee/Be!

Fact File

The most popular code today is Short Message Service (SMS). That's the name for text messaging on mobile phones.
TXTMSGRQL*

I'm so common

Knowing how often a letter is used can help you work out a code. The eight letters most used in English are: E, T, O, A, N, I, R, S, in that order.

It's a living!

The Egyptian hieroglyph for the word "trouble" has a crocodile creeping in it.

Navy code books were covered in lead. This made them heavy. If a ship was captured, the code book was thrown overboard to sink to the bottom of the sea.

*Answer: Text messages are cool.

Glossary

archaeologists people who study ancient cultures by digging up and describing their remains

cipher a system of changing text to keep its meaning secret

code a system of signs or symbols, each with a meaning

cryptographer a person who makes codes (encodes) and breaks them (decodes)

decoded when a coded message has been converted to plain text

encoding converting plain text to a different form, using a code

key symbols that control the code or cipher, known only to the sender and receiver

random without order or pattern

scytale a baton or stick used with a belt or strip of paper to send secret messages

Index